The Punta Gorda Book of Values

Martha R. Bireda, Ph.D.
Jaha Cummings

Blue Ocean Press

Published by: Blue Ocean Press

USA Office
P.O. Box 510818
Punta Gorda, FL 33951 USA

Japan Office
6F & 7F TOC Daiichi Bldg.
1-8-3 Shibuya, Shibuya-ku
Tokyo, Japan 150-0002

URL: http://www.blueoceanpublications.com
Email: director@aoishima-research.org

ISBN: 978-4-902837-31-5

Cover Picture: Martha Baker Long Andrews

TABLE OF CONTENTS

THANK YOU

My sincere thank you to those who helped make this book possible. First, thank you to Yolanda Marion for all your assistance, especially for taking and choosing photographs. Thank you to the *Charlotte Sun* newspaper, and especially to Janine Smith for the willingness to let me read the very "delicate" old copies of the Punta Gorda Herald. Thank you to Bill MacDonald for his assistance in finding microfiche of old editions of the Punta Gorda Herald, and special thanks to Richard Carey for assistance with graphic work.

INTRODUCTION TO THE PUNTA GORDA BOOK OF VALUES

Punta Gorda has been described as "The Little Town that Unity Built" characterized as having a "unique sociology" due to its biracial settlement and development. Punta Gorda was built by its founders on the principles of mutual respect and shared prosperity.

Punta Gorda was founded by both black and white pioneers, despite Florida's Jim Crow laws. Together they created a society where all members of their community could thrive. This book is the story of the values that sustained Punta Gorda's early African American pioneers.

PUNTA GORDA: A DISTINCT & UNIQUE HISTORY

JIM CROW ERA

By 1885, Jim Crow was fully entrenched in Florida's laws and customs. Even so, four African American landholders and voters were part of the 34 men who incorporated the City of Punta Gorda in 1887. An African American Postmaster was appointed in 1889. Blacks and whites worked together to tame the Southwest Florida frontier and to create a thriving community. Punta Gorda, exceptional in its race relations, was one of the first school districts to voluntarily integrate in 1964. This biracial unity created a "shared prosperity" experienced by all residents despite the presence of Jim Crow.

WHAT WAS JIM CROW?

- State laws enacted in the 1800s by lawmakers bitter about the end of slavery, loss of the Civil War, and the advances made by African Americans during Reconstruction.
- A system of segregation and discrimination that barred African Americans from a status equal to that of white Americans, which operated primarily, but not exclusively, in the southern and border states between 1877 and the mid-1960s.

MODEL COMMUNITY

Punta Gorda's history serves as a model for our country in demonstrating the power of societal unity. Based on values of unity and shared prosperity, Punta Gorda was an environment in which all of its citizens could thrive economically. For example, George Brown, a local African American businessman, owned a successful shipyard operation which provided employment to residents during the Great Depression, a time in which many other communities suffered from widespread joblessness.

It was only in conforming to the national trend to implement Urban Renewal policies in the 1960s that led to the demise of Punta Gorda's thriving African American business district. The golden age of historic African American business districts almost uniformly came to an end because of the Urban Renewal policies implemented between 1949 into the mid-1970s.

PUNTA GORDA VALUES

The traditional values held by the pioneers that settled Punta Gorda enabled the community to survive and to thrive. These values passed generation to generation from 1885 to the late 1960s were learned by one of the authors herself as a girl growing up in Punta Gorda.

Using old photographs and newspaper articles, the eight core values learned by the children of Punta Gorda are shared with young readers ages 9-13. The values taught in Punta Gorda are typical of those held by the descendants of enslaved people who established communities after the turn of the century. This book, originally written for the youth of Punta Gorda, has much to teach youth everywhere about values and character.

DEDICATION

This book is dedicated to Bernice Andrews Russell, social activist, humanitarian, African American historian, and the inspiration for the Blanchard House Museum of African American History and Culture of Charlotte County, Florida.

BERNICE ANDREWS RUSSELL

Bernice Andrews Russell was a proud woman. She was proud of her ancestry, her heritage, and her community. This pride inspired her to want to preserve the memories that shaped her life. Her greatest desire was that the African American children in Punta Gorda would "know who they were" so that they too could share her sense of pride.

WHY WE SHOULD LEARN ABOUT VALUES

Values are what a group of people feel are important. Our values help us to decide what is right or wrong. They guide our actions. They are like signs on the highway; they point out the right direction in which we are to go. Our values help to determine our character. When we say that a person has good character, we are talking about their values.

This book is about values. One way in which we can learn about values is to study history and learn about the values of historical figures. In this book, we will learn about the values of a group of African American pioneers who settled in southwest Florida in 1885 and helped to establish the town of Trabue, later called Punta Gorda, on the Charlotte Harbor.

Just 20 years after the end of slavery, these African Americans built a thriving community. They were men and women of good character. Their values helped them to be successful and in being integral to the settlement of Punta Gorda and Charlotte County. These African American pioneers were guided by eight values.

What do you think these values were?
In this book, we will read about the values learned by the children who grew up in Punta Gorda and how these values were passed on to four generations.

NEW WORDS

Some words that you read in this book will be new to you. When you come across a word that you do not know, look it up in the dictionary. Our language is always changing and has changed much since the early 1900s. Some words and phrases that you will read in the old newspaper articles will not be familiar to you. In fact, you may find them to be funny. One word that you will see used in the old newspaper articles is "colored." This word was used to describe black people or African Americans before and during the 1900s. When you come across old words or phrases, ask an elder to help you understand their meaning.

AFRICAN AMERICAN LIFE IN THE LATE 18TH AND EARLY 19TH CENTURIES

The values of the African American pioneers who settled in Punta Gorda came from two sources. They were both the values of their ancestors who came from Africa and the values adopted by African Americans to help them cope with the hard times they experienced as slaves and as freedmen.

The African American pioneers were either born enslaved themselves or the children of parents who were slaves. These pioneers, like other African Americans, were very hopeful that they would enjoy the same rights and freedoms as other Americans after the end of Civil War and slavery. For more than ten years after the slaves were freed and during Reconstruction, schools were established for the ex-slaves, and African American politicians were elected to office.

In fact, two of the African American pioneers living in Punta Gorda had been politicians during the Reconstruction era. Owen B. Armstrong, a teacher and carpenter, had been a delegate to the 1868 Constitutional Convention in Florida and served as a Leon County (Florida) commissioner from 1869-1870. He was also one of the four African American men to participate in Punta Gorda's first election. He was an active Republican until 1904.

Robert Meacham had been one of the most important Reconstruction leaders in Florida. He was a delegate to the 1868 Constitutional Convention and served in the Florida Senate from Jefferson County for ten years. While in the Florida Legislature, Robert Meacham helped establish the state's public education system.

Mr. Meacham, a minister, who had helped to establish AME churches in Florida, was the postmaster of Punta Gorda from 1889-1891. He was forced to resign in 1892.

During the Reconstruction period, 1865-1876, the laws provided protection for the Freedmen, but when Reconstruction ended in 1877, life again became very difficult for African Americans. African American politicians were forced out of office, African Americans lost the right to vote, lost their jobs, and faced extreme violence directed toward them. Many of the pioneers who settled in Punta Gorda came from northern Florida and from other southern states such as Georgia, South Carolina, and Alabama where life for African Americans was especially hard. They came to what was still considered to be the "frontier" of southwest Florida to escape the prejudice and violence they faced elsewhere.

Robert Meachum was appointed as Postmaster on

January 24, 1890

THE VALUES OF PUNTA GORDA

- Spirituality
- Family
- Children
- Education
- Work
- Self-reliance
- Community
- Equality

THE VALUE OF SPIRITUALITY

BELIEF: God will provide.

A thatched palmetto hut like this one was the site of the first worship service held in Punta Gorda.

Faith in God was one of the most strongly held values of the pioneers who settled in Punta Gorda. They believed that God would "make a way for them out of no way" and help them to survive however hard the times were that they faced.

Dan Smith, a member of the survey team that came to *Trabue* in 1885, organized the first religious service, which was comprised of both Christians and Jews. After the train tracks for the Florida Southern Railway were completed and the first train arrived, Smith held the church service under a thatched palmetto hut. The first congregation was made up of blacks and whites of all denominations.

The establishment of Bethel African Methodist Episcopal Church was the result of this first religious service. After Dan Smith married Louisa Evans, a Baptist, he along with Caine Dorsey founded St. Mark Progressive Baptist Church. The value of spirituality was so important, that by 1916, there were four African American churches in downtown Punta Gorda.

Sunday was a very special day in that much of the day was devoted to serving God. Most people attended Sunday School and Morning Service, went home to have Sunday dinner by 2:00, then came back for Evening Service by 6:00 P.M.

They also attended a weekly prayer meeting and Bible study. The church not only served the spiritual needs of the people but the social needs as well. The church provided for the needy in all ways.

THE PUNTA GORDA HERALD

April 24, 1913

Punta Gorda colored people are to have another church building. The members of the M.E. Church North are to build. E. Green of the board of trustees has placed an order for the materials and the contract has been let to M.J. Martin.

November 27, 1915

A big revival meeting lasting several weeks was concluded Sunday night at the A.M.E. church (colored), and as a result Pastor H.W. Gray says thirty-three new members have been added to the roll of the church and two to the Baptist church. Of those joining, the A.M.E. church, twenty-eight are to be baptized Sunday; fifteen to be immersed and thirteen sprinkled. The immersion will take place at an early-hour of the forenoon in the Bay just north of the boat sheds.

WHAT DID I LEARN?

1. Why do you think the value of "faith in God" was so important to the people of Punta Gorda?

2. How did the people of Punta Gorda demonstrate their strong faith in God?

3. What does "God will provide" mean to you?

4. Is the value of "faith in God" important to you? Why? or Why not?

LIVING HISTORY ASSIGNMENT

1. Interview an elder; ask them to tell you about the first churches that were established in Punta Gorda or in your community. What denominations were those churches?

2. Write a paper telling how the churches of the early 1900s are the same as and different from churches today.

THE VALUE OF FAMILY

BELIEF: When one has, all have.

Three generations. Mrs. Cornelius Ponder, with her daughter and granddaughter.

Next to God, the family was the greatest source of strength for the early settlers. The Punta Gorda community was made up of strong families that worked together to provide a better life for all. The pioneers that settled in Punta Gorda understood the value of family. During slavery, many African American families were torn apart. Children were sold away from parents, and parents from children. After slavery ended, husbands and wives searched for each other, and parents went to find their children. The experiences of slavery made family ties very important to African Americans.

To the people of Punta Gorda, family did not only mean a mother, father, and children. Family meant grandparents, aunts, uncles, cousins and even people who were not blood kin. In Punta Gorda, people considered "godparents" and "play" brothers and sisters to also be a part of the family.

Family members depended upon each other. They lived together, worked together, shared food, and money. Families also played together. The whole family had picnics, went to baseball games and on "excursions" together. As soon as they were able, the men who settled in Punta Gorda sent for their parents, sisters, and brothers to join them. As family members "got on their feet," they in turn sent for another relative. During the 1940s when many of the African American young people who grew up in Punta Gorda went up north in search of better jobs, they stayed with relatives who had gone before them. Like their ancestors had done many years before, "when they got on their feet," they sent for younger brothers and sisters to join them.

Older brothers and sisters also worked so that younger ones could finish high school and go off to college. As each brother or sister graduated from college, they were expected to help the next one. In some ways, the college education of one belonged to the whole family.

Saving money to buy land and build a house of their own was a major goal of most of the families that lived in Punta Gorda. By 1900, only 15 years after the first African Americans arrived in Punta Gorda, 37% already owned their own homes.

By working together, the families were also able to establish businesses. One of the most successful families in business was headed by Mack and Illinois Gollman. For many years, the Gollman family-owned businesses served the community and provided jobs for residents. These businesses included the Royal Palm Ballroom, a restaurant, a café, a bar, and several rental houses.

The Royal Palm Ballroom was part of a network of African American-owned establishments that featured entertainment known as the "Chitlin' Circuit". The "Chitlin' Circuit" was a group of performance venues located mostly in the South that were safe and acceptable places for African American musicians and entertainers to perform during Jim Crow.

Nathaniel Gollman had a jazz band called "Nat and His Florida Stompers" who played at Gollman's as well as throughout southwest Florida.

On Friday & Saturday nights, people who came from Fort Myers, Arcadia, and other surrounding towns to "Down the Street," (Cochran Street Business District) where the African American businesses thrived, to enjoy nightlife in Punta Gorda. Most enjoyed the music of the Florida Stompers at the Royal Palm Ballroom. The Royal Palm Ballroom was also used by the neighborhood children on weekends as a roller rink.

Gollman Family Home

The Gollman Family Home was one of the three two-story houses in the neighborhood. Another was owned by James and Queen Andrews. Due to Urban Renewal, none of these houses remain.

THE PUNTA GORDA HERALD

June 7, 1895

A special train will leave Punta Gorda at 6 o'clock next Thursday morning, June 13, for Tampa and Picnic Island. The fare will be $1 for adults and 50cents for children. Two front coaches will be especially for colored passengers. Cooling refreshments will be served aboard the cars. The train will arrive at Tampa at 11:00 A.M.

March 14, 1918

Ben Coleman, well known colored man, has the lumber on the ground to build a $1200.00 cottage in the neighborhood of the colored public school.

WHAT DID I LEARN?

1. What does "when one has, all have" mean to you?

2. What did the word "family" mean to the pioneers?

3. Why was being a part of a strong family so important to the pioneers?

4. Why was buying land and owning a home important to the residents of Punta Gorda?

5. One of the pioneer families were the Haynes'. Mr. Willie and Mrs. Annie Mae Haynes believed that "if our children can look up to us, they will never look down on themselves." Why do you think that they believed this? How do you think this belief affected their children and who they grew up to be?

LIVING HISTORY ASSIGNMENT

1. Interview a member of one of the pioneer families that still lives in Punta Gorda. Ask them to tell you about their family. If you do not live in Punta Gorda, interview a member of one of the pioneer families from your area. Ask them to tell you about their family.

2. Draw a family tree for one of the pioneer families, or for one of the elders in your community.

3. Talk to an elder in your family; ask them to help you to draw a family tree for your family. Ask them when your family first came to the community in which you now live. Ask him or her to tell you about the early experiences of your family.

THE VALUE OF CHILDREN

Belief: Children are our future.

Annual Spring Festival

Baker Academy-1950s

Children were very special in the Punta Gorda community. All of the adults wanted to provide a better life for the children than the one they had known growing up. In Punta Gorda, all adults were responsible for teaching and guiding children. The children understood that they must respect and obey all adults in the community.

Much of what was taught and expected of children living in Punta Gorda was known as "home training." Home training had to do mostly with learning respect and proper manners. The most important rules of home training were:

1. Respect yourself.
2. Respect your family.
3. Respect the elderly.

A family's name was very important, and children were taught and expected not to do anything to bring shame to themselves or to the family. Respect for the elders was most important. In the African tradition, ancestors are very highly respected and since elders are considered to be closest to the ancestors, they are very special. To talk back to, roll one's eyes at, or suck one's teeth in the presence of an elder could get a child into big trouble. Children could not listen to or interrupt the conversations of elders. Most important, whenever a child saw an elder, they were to speak to them.

Good manners were expected of children at all times. There were always women in the Punta Gorda community who took responsibility for teaching etiquette and manners to the children During the 1950s and 1960s, "Miss Edna" (Mrs. Edna Thomas) hosted teas and dinner parties so that children in Punta Gorda could learn the "social graces."

In the community, through church and school, the children of Punta Gorda learned pride in their race and heritage. In both church and school, the children learned the African oral tradition.

At church, children had to take part in religious programs and pageants. Every child in the community, from the oldest to the youngest, had to memorize and recite a Christmas and Easter speech.

In school, students also learned to "stand and deliver" as part of the oral tradition. The school gave monthly recitals in the community in which all grades took part and a program at the end of each school year to celebrate the closing of school and to honor the graduates.

"Giving back" was a value learned by all of the children who grew up in Punta Gorda. They knew that like their parents and other adults in the community that when they grew up, they too would have to contribute to the community by "serving" in some way.

Children followed in their parent's footsteps. Archie Bailey, Annie Mae Haynes, and Martha Andrews started the local branch of the NAACP in 1933. The next generation, Berlin Bailey, Booker T. Haynes, Sr., and Bernice Andrews Russell all took an active role in the civil rights movement and community affairs.

Dinner party hosted by "Miss Edna".

1950s

THE PUNTA GORDA HERALD

May 8, 1913

Tuesday night, the boys of the 4th and 5th grades will present a Mock trial, the famous watermelon case. Wednesday night, the girls will Render a very beautiful cantata, "A Dream of Fairyland." These exercises will take place at Miller's Hall. A small admission charge to cover expenses.

B.J. Baker, Principal

COLORED SCHOOL TO CLOSE

The closing exercises of the colored public school will begin Sunday, May 12, at St. Marks Progressive Baptist Church at 2:30 p.m. A short program will be rendered by the grades consisting of songs and readings. There will be two graduates, Olivia A. White and Carrie L. Smith. The Baccalaureate sermon will be delivered by Rev. M.L. Cherry. Wednesday and Thursday nights, 15th and 16th insts., concerts will be rendered at the Masonic Temple. All are cordially invited to the exercises.___B.J. Baker, Principal

May 20, 1915

Colored School To Close

The closing of the colored public school will begin Sunday, May 23rd. This feature of the exercises will be conducted at St. Mark Progressive Baptist Church, consisting of a short program rendered by the pupils of the 5th,6th and 7th grades, followed by the annual sermon by Rev. Maj. L. Cherry. Exercises will begin at 2:30 p.m.

Song___Holy, Holy.

Responsive Reading.

Reading of the Scripture___Rev. M. L. Cherry

Invocation____Rev. H.W. Gary.

Song___Never Say Fail.

Paper___"What are we living for?" Edith Dwight

Recitation___The Lost Chord, Olivia White.

Paper____Time to Cultivate Honor. J.C. Coleman

Vesper Song____School.

Paper___"Is this a Christian nation?" by Frank Andrews.

Duet___Summer Blossoms, Edith Dwight, Olivia White

Annual Sermon___Rev. M.L. Cherry

All invited, seats free.

The annual concert will be given at Miller's Hall, Wednesday and Thursday nights, May 26 and 27.

____B.J. Baker, Principal

WHAT DID I LEARN?

1. What is "home training"?

2. What was expected of children growing up in Punta Gorda? What do you think of those expectations?

3. Why was it important for the children of Punta Gorda to participate in plays and programs? In what ways are you learning to "stand and deliver"?

4. What does the school closing program in the newspaper tell you about the values of the students who attended the colored school.

5. What does it mean to "give back"?

6. How would your life be different if you had grown up in Punta Gorda during the early 1900s?

LIVING HISTORY ASSIGNMENT

1. Interview an elder; talk to him or her about how bringing up children has changed from the "old days" to now.

2. Interview your grandparents or other elders, find out what games children played during the early 1900s; see if you can re-create some of the same games and toys.

Mrs. Cornelius Ponder

MRS. CORNELIUS PONDER

(1870-1934)

Mrs. Ponder believed that being a midwife was a God-given talent and that helping to bring life into the world was one of the greatest gifts one could give.

Mrs. Ponder was one of the first midwives in Punta Gorda and is the only midwife listed in the 1900 census. Mrs. Ponder was very religious and depended upon God to help her to do her work.

For Mrs. Ponder, being a midwife was "a labor of love." Many times, she was not paid; however, she always gave the best of care to all of her patients.

Most of the children who grew up in Punta Gorda were delivered by Mrs. Ponder.

1. What is “a labor of love”?

2. What were the values of greatest importance to Mrs. Ponder?

THE VALUE OF EDUCATION

BELIEF: You have to get an education to be successful in life.

Students of old colored school.

Early 1900s

The pioneers of Punta Gorda placed a very high value on education. All of the parents wanted their children to have more education than them. They wanted their children to go as far as they could in school. Finishing high school was felt to be absolutely necessary and going on to college was very desirable. Each generation that grew up in Punta Gorda was more educated than the one before.

Knowledge and learning are values of the African culture that is the heritage of the pioneers of Punta Gorda. Before Africans were taken as slaves and brought to the New World, there had been great universities in Africa, such as the University of Sankoré. The pioneers learned the value of education from the stories told by their parents and grandparents who had been enslaved. Although slaves were punished for learning to read and write, many took the risk and learned anyway.

The pioneers believed that "an education is the one thing that no one can take away from you." Even adults who had not learned to read and write were eager to do so. By 1900, just 35 years after the end of slavery and 15 years after Punta Gorda was settled, 70% of the African American residents of Punta Gorda could read and 60% could read and write. Dan Smith, community leader, while he was so gifted in math that he was able to lead the team of surveyors that brought the railroad from Bartow to Punta Gorda, did not learn to read and write until taught how to by his wife Louisa.

The first school for African Americans in Punta Gorda was a little private Adventist school. Mrs. Giles taught students on the porch of her home. Parents paid 15 cents per week to have her teach their children. "When the water came out of the Peace River, the men would piggy back their children to the porch."

In 1902, the African American citizens of Punta Gorda founded a public school for "colored" children. They collected money, bought land, and worked together to build the school. Dan Smith was sent to find a teacher. Benjamin Baker was the first teacher of the colored school. Having a school for colored children was so important that two adults, Dan Smith and Alex Stephens, attended school with children so that the community would have the quota of students needed for the County to pay for a teacher for the colored school.

Because of the State of Florida's Jim Crow laws, schools were segregated, and the colored school did not receive as much money as the white school to operate. African American students often had no books or old books and fewer supplies than the white school. The colored school only went to the eighth grade. Parents made great sacrifices so that their children could finish high school. Some parents worked hard to pay tuition for their children to attend a private boarding school, while most lived away from home with relatives in towns where they could attend a colored high school. The African American residents of Punta Gorda believed that every child could learn; there were no excuses for failing to go as far in school as possible.

Not only learning to read and write, but being an outstanding student was very important. When African American students in Punta Gorda made the Honor Roll, their names were published in the Punta Gorda Herald weekly newspaper for all to see. To be on the Honor Roll brought great pride to the students, their parents, and the whole community.

THE PUNTA GORDA HERALD

November 3, 1922

Students who qualified for the honor roll at Baker Academy:

Lily Mae Reddish

Huldy Andrews

Odessa Reddish

Bernice Andrews

Shellie Lee Slay

Catherine Andrews

Mayola Ponder

Emma Bagley

Lillian Gollman

Ida Mae Scott

Frances Roberts

Albert Williams

THE PUNTA GORDA HERALD

December 19, 1902

Rev. L.A. Johnson and A.B. Coleman, two public-spirited colored citizens, have raised $50 with which they have bought four lots just north of the Colored Baptist Church, whereupon to build a school house.

August 20, 1908

The Negroes have a good public school with one teacher and about 35 students.

May 8, 1913

The Punta Gorda Colored School will close May 18th. The Graduating exercises will take place at the A.M.E. Church, May 18, 7:30P.M. Baccalaureate service by Rev. M.L. Cherry, this city. The public has been cordially invited. Seats free.

October 13, 1922

Baker's Academy, the local public school for colored pupils, with three teachers is making good progress. The enrollment is 95.

WHAT DID I LEARN?

1. Why was getting an education so important to the African American residents of Punta Gorda?

2. What hardships did African Americans face in getting educated? Why did they not get discouraged?

3. How did educating their children help the Punta Gorda community to become successful?

4. How was being a student in the early 1900s different from being a student now?

LIVING HISTORY ASSIGNMENT

1. Talk to an elder who attended the Baker Academy, or another African American who attended segregated schools. Do a report on what school was like in the "old days." Ask about the subjects that students took, what teachers were like; and what was expected of students.

2. Charlotte County will soon be celebrating the 60th anniversary of the voluntary desegregation of Charlotte High School in 1964. What is the meaning of "segregation"; "desegregation"; "voluntary segregation"? Interview black and white elders to learn what the first days of going to school together was like.

3. Write a report about the meaning of the 1954 United States Supreme Court decision outlawing school segregation.

Professor Benjamin J. Baker

BENJAMIN JOSHUA BAKER

(1872-1942)

When Benjamin Baker was born, slavery had only been abolished for eight years. Despite the risk of punishment, his parents had learned to read. They promised each other that their son, Benjamin, would learn to read, write, count, and speak correctly.

Benjamin Baker did not go to school until he was ten years old, and then, only for two or three months each semester, because he had to work in the fields. By the time he was 19, however, he passed the test to become a teacher.

In 1902, Benjamin Baker was hired to teach at the Colored School in Punta Gorda. He was a very religious man who had high moral principles. Even though he was a very strict teacher and principal, he was loved by all of his students who called him "Fess."

1. What values do you believe guided Benjamin Baker?

THE VALUE OF WORK

BELIEF: A colored man has to work twice as hard to succeed.

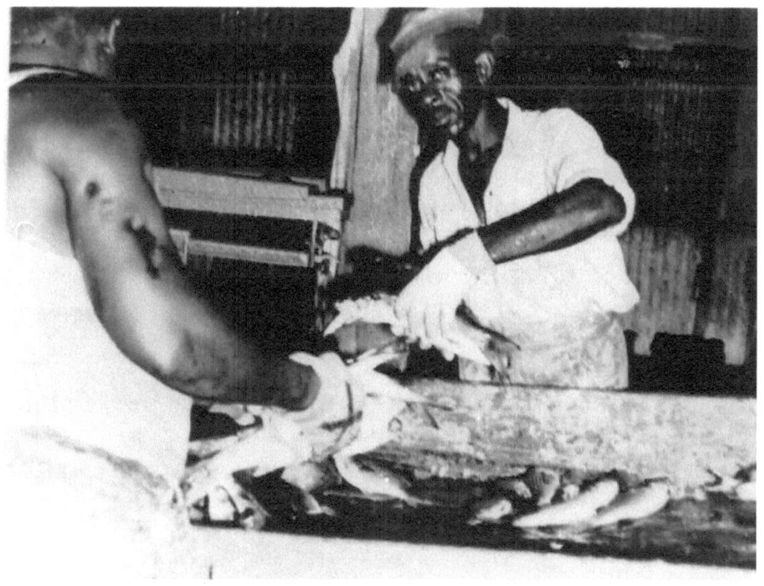

Andrew "Mullet" Owens

One of the best workers at the Punta Gorda Fish Company.

The men and women who settled in Punta Gorda worked hard to build a better life for themselves and their children. They did all the kinds of work that were necessary in Punta Gorda. Many men worked as day laborers who helped to lay the brick streets and build the "big hotel." Some worked in the phosphate mills and turpentine stills. Others were skilled workers such as carpenters, draymen, machinists, and shipwrights. Often the women were employed as washerwomen and cooks.

Most men were employed in the fishing industry. In the early days, fishing -- commercial and "sports"-- was the major industry in Punta Gorda. The African American fishermen fished in small boats called "sharpies." They fished every day from before sunrise to after twilight, what they called "dark to dark." They would spend up to five days out fishing, they would ice their fish and bring them back to the fish house for packing. African Americans worked on the docks packing the fish to be transported by train or truck to many other states.

The African Americans who settled in Punta Gorda were not only interested in working hard but achieving as well. They worked twice as hard as other workers and took great pride in their work. Many times, the African American workers would be described as the "fastest" or "best" at the work that they did.

THE PUNTA GORDA HERALD

September 16, 1915

Peter W. Miller, a popular colored citizen, after doing very satisfactory work for the government for nine months at Sparrow's Point, Md., came home last week and was warmly greeted by his many friends.

January 30, 1919

That well-known colored citizen, Chas. L. Pratt, has decided to return to his old profession of tarpon guide. He has had years of successful experience in the work, for which he is getting his boat and other equipment ready.

January 29, 1904

The sharpie "D.C. Smith" named for her owner and builder, who is an industrious colored man, has proved to be one of the best boats of the fishing fleet. She is navigated by her owner and is bringing in lots of fish.

September 19, 1904

The yacht "Ethel Q." has just come off the ways of Cleveland where she underwent an overhaul. She is now in "apple pie order" for business. Her skipper is Capt. Green, the well-known colored seaman.

WHAT DID I LEARN?

1. We often see the words "expert," "best," and "industrious" used to describe the pioneers. What does this tell you about the values and character of these men and women?

2. Why did the pioneers believe they had to work twice as hard as others (whites) to succeed? Why did they not get discouraged?

LIVING HISTORY ASSIGNMENT

1. Interview an elder who can tell you about the commercial and sport-fishing industry in early Punta Gorda. Ask him or her about Mr. Andrew "Mullet" Owens, Mr. Gaitor, the fastest oyster opener, Mr. Ollie Washington, and Mr. Bud Whitehead, two of the best tarpon guides. If you do not live in Punta Gorda, interview an elder about a dynamic industry that existed in your community in the past.

2. "Sharpie Town" was the area in which the African American fishermen lived. It was located on the river across from where the hospital in Punta Gorda stands now. First, what is a "sharpie"? Do some investigation, find out what you can about "Sharpie Town."

THE VALUE OF SELF-RELIANCE

BELIEF: We must do for ourselves.

The Cleveland Marine Steamways

Owned by George Brown

The settlers of Punta Gorda not only worked hard at their jobs but even harder to establish businesses of their own. They believed in not just finding a job but in creating jobs for themselves and other people in the community.

In 1902, African Americans owned a hotel (the Ingram Hotel), a rooming house (Miss Carrie Washington), a barber shop (The Star Shaving Parlor, A.B. Coleman) and a grocery store (O.B. Armstrong). By 1927, 20 African American-owned businesses were listed in the Punta Gorda City Directory.

They built businesses to meet the needs of the people living in Punta Gorda. There were grocery stores, restaurants, dry cleaners, rooming houses, a gas station, a drugstore, and even a Venetian blind factory. Some businesses were smaller and run by one person. There was someone in the Punta Gorda community from which residents could buy ice and wood.

The pioneers also established lodges and organizations to help residents when they became ill or when a family member died. Some of the dues that members paid to their lodges were used to pay the cost of their funeral when they died; these were called "burial societies." In the Punta Gorda community, most people belonged to one or more of these lodges and organizations: the Masons, the Oddfellows, the Herods of Jericho, the Eastern Stars, the Lily Whites, and the American Woodmen. All these organizations were also known as "self-help" organizations.

A REPRODUCTION OF THE LISTINGS

FOR THE AFRICAN-AMERCAN OWNED BUSINESSES

AS INDICATED IN THE

POLKS

CHARLOTTE COUNTY

Classified Business Directory

1927-28

R.L. Polk & Co., Publishers

Barbers

Gollman Mack (c) es Cochran 1 s of Hargreaves av

Billiard and Pocket Billiard Rooms

Alex Stephens (c) ws Cochran 1 s of Virginia

SAMUEL HR (c) ws Cochran 1 s of Olympia 1 s of Olympia av (See page 13)

Boarding Houses

Gollman Mack (c) 352 Cochran

Clothes Pressers, Cleaners and Repairers

City Pressing Club (c) ns Charlotte av 1 e of Milus

NuWay Pressing Club (c) es Cochran 2 n of Virginia av

Walker H W (c) ns Charlotte av 1 e of Milus

Electricians

Bailey, Archie (c; electl) ss Virginia av 1 e of Wood

Filling Stations

SAMUEL, H R (c), Cooper at A C L R R (See Page 13)

Furnished Rooms

SAMUELS HOTEL (c), Cooper at A C L R R (See Page 13)

Gasoline and Oil Service Stations

SAMUELS H R (c), Cooper at A C L R R (See Page 13)

Grocers – Retail

Dorsey A K (c) cc Charlotte av 2 e of Milus

Sanders Levi (c) 336 Cochran

Hotels

SAMUELS HOTEL (c), Cooper at A C L R R (See page 13)

Meats - Retail

Samuels Levi (c) Cochran nw cor Virginia av

Rentals

SAMUELS H R (c), Cooper at A C L R R (See Page 13)

Restaurants

Busy Bee Café (c) ws Cochran 1 s of Hargreaves

Shine & Baykin (c) 313 E Olympia av

Silver Moon Café (c) ws Cochran 2 n of Virginia av

Wood Dealers

Bailey Archie (c) ss Virginia av 1 e of Wood

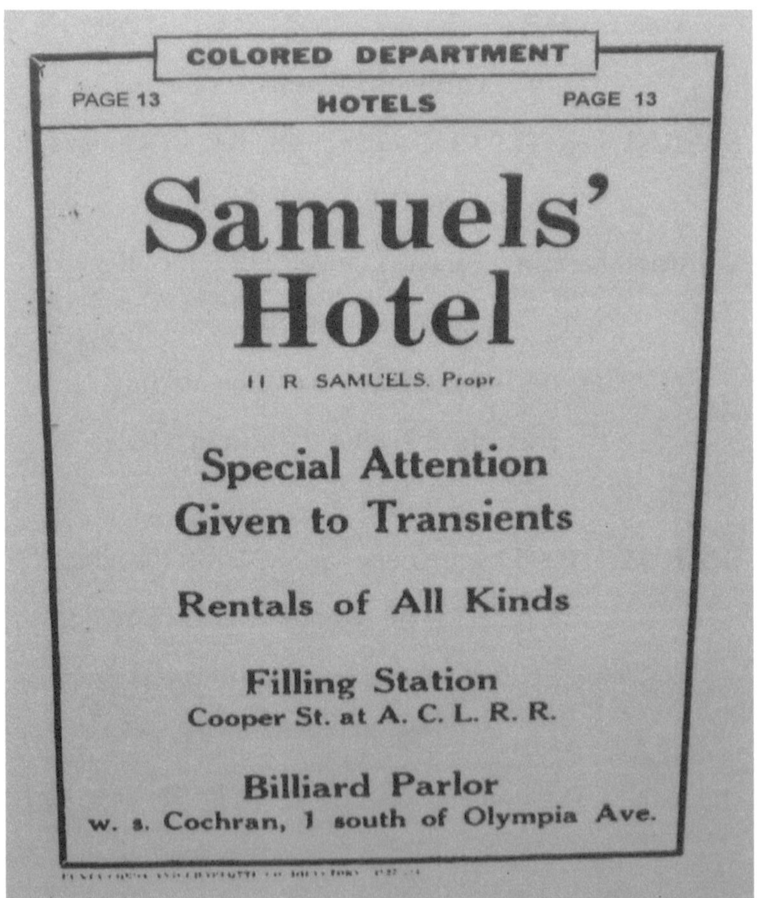

Henry Samuels

THE PUNTA GORDA HERALD

February 6, 1913

The framework for the new hall for the colored Oddfellows of this city has been erected and the building will be rushed to completion as soon as further materials are received. It occupies a portion in the Eastern edge of the town and is being built under the supervision of contractor M.J. Martin

April 18, 1918

The ladies of the Colored Peoples Auxiliary of the Punta Gorda Red Cross are busy trying to get the boys of Punta Gorda ready for camp.

Our membership is twelve and we would be glad if other friends would join us.

A. Ambrose, Sec.

May 9, 1918

Mrs. Charles Pratt went to Jacksonville as a delegate to the annual meeting of the grand lodge of the Household of Ruth I.O.O.F. jurisdiction of colored people.

THE PUNTA GORDA HERALD

January 15, 1904

STAR SHAVING PARLOR

A. B. Coleman, Proprietor

HAIR CUTTING, SHAVING,

SHAMPOOING AND TREATING

OF ALL FORMS OF SCALP DISEASES

First Class Work. Satisfaction Guaranteed.

CHARCOAL FOR SALE.

February 6, 1908

E. Ward, colored, wishes it known that he has a fine new surrey, with a fast, gentle horse, for taking people anywhere in-or about town.

September 10, 1908

George Brown, the popular colored stevedore and expert 1908 machinist, is putting in up-to-date steam ways at Cleveland, of which he will take personal charge. This means he has given up his job at Port Inglis and will remain at Cleveland.

WHAT DID I LEARN?

1. Why was it so important for African Americans to own their own businesses during the early 1900s?

2. Why were the lodges and organizations called "self-help" societies?

LIVING HISTORY ASSIGNMENT

1. Read the 1927 Punta Gorda Business Directory. Write a report on the types of businesses that African Americans owned. Interview an elder and then write a report about the African American-owned businesses that existed historically along Cochran Street (presently Dr. Martin Luther King Jr, Boulevard) until urban renewal policies were implemented in 1968 that led to the eventual decline of this historic business district. If you do not live in Punta Gorda, interview an elder and write a report about the African American-owned businesses that existed in your community before urban renewal were implemented between the late 1950s and early 1970s.

2. Interview an elder and then write a report about the early lodges and organizations established by the pioneers in Punta Gorda.

George Brown at age 75, holding
a neighbor's son, John Howell Teter, Jr.

GEORGE BROWN

(1868-1951)

George Brown, a carpenter, came from Charleston, Carolina to Cleveland, Florida in 1891. He brought a crew of other African Americans with him to build drying bins and barges for the DeSoto Phosphate Mining Company.

In 1897, Mr. Brown started his own shipyard, called Cleveland Marine Steam Ways. Mr. Brown's steam way was the first and largest in Southwest Florida. The Steam Ways serviced both cargo ships and pleasure yachts.

Mr. Brown was a major landowner, at one time owning half of the land in Punta Gorda. He was active in civic affairs and was known to give generously to churches and charities in the area.

In 1927, Mr. Brown sold the land to the newly formed Charlotte County on which the old courthouse and mural dedicated to him now stands.

Mr. Brown was a major employer in Charlotte County, hiring both black and white workers, and paying equal wages for equal work. He is considered to be Florida's first "equal opportunity" employer.

WHAT DID YOU LEARN?

1. What values do you believe guided Mr. Brown?

2. What is an "equal opportunity" employer?

LIVING HISTORY ASSIGNMENT

1. On the following page is a mural dedicated to Mr. Brown, showing both his community and work life. If possible, visit the mural; what values do see reflected in the mural describing Mr. Brown?

The George Brown Mural

THE VALUE OF COMMUNITY

BELIEF: The whole is greater than the parts.

Five of the seven Bailey brothers

whom all served in WWII.

The Punta Gorda community was like one big family. Each person, even children, had to do their part to make the community work. Families in Punta Gorda shared the vegetables grown in gardens as well as oranges, grapefruits, mangoes, and guavas from trees. The fishermen shared their catches. The men helped each other build houses, the women made quilts together, and those with cars transported those without.

The community not only worked together but played together as well. On Saturday nights, there were plays, concerts, and boxing matches at Miller's Hall. Churches sponsored picnics and hayrides.

On Saturday and Sunday afternoons, the whole community turned out to watch the local team play baseball. There were also outings by boat to the nearby islands.

The pioneers were not only concerned about African American community, but the whole community of Punta Gorda, as well. From the time that the first seven African American men arrived, they were active in civic affairs in Punta Gorda. Four African American men, O.B. Armstrong, Elihu Justice, E.C. Jackson, and Sam Kenady signed the papers to incorporate the city of Punta Gorda in 1887. The pioneers volunteered their time and money to help build the new town.

PUNTA GORDA HERALD THE PUNTA

May 25, 1894

The Florida Southern brought down quite a large excursion of colored people last Monday from Bartow and other points to the north. The principal attraction while here was a baseball game between the "Ninos" of Bartow and Punta Gorda.

December 26, 1902

Our colored people had a big Christmas. They began on Tuesday with an entertainment by the Dixie Comedy Company in the Colored Masonic Hall and followed up with private social affairs every night since.

June 15, 1916

Punta Gorda colored citizens entertained a large number of the colored citizens of Fort Myers who came up on the special excursion Monday. In a baseball game in the afternoon Punta Gorda girls beat the Ft. Myers girls and the Ft. Myers men were the winners over the Punta Gorda men.

The pioneers volunteered their time and money to help to build the new town.

THE PUNTA GORDA HERALD

September 24, 1908

The colored citizens of Punta Gorda held a meeting at their Masonic Hall and agreed to help build the wharf. Those contributing included: S.P. Andrews, Lem Jackson, D.C. Smith, John Smith, C.L. Pratt, P.W. Miller, John Davis, E. Ward, T.W. Sanders, Charles Smith, Howard Lewis, Louis Zanders, Sam Kenady, Geo. Brown, J.J. Mitchell, A.B. Coleman, Frank Sanders, John McGee.

October 1, 1908

A large force went down the bay for piling Monday morning September and so Punta Gorda's public dock has started: the following colored citizens went: Lem Jackson, E. Ward, H. Lewis, L. Zanders, C.H. Smith, Ben Andrews.

October 30, 1919

The Colored People Civic Association last week donated $8.00 to the fund to build a fountain to the new artesian well at the intersection of Marion Avenue and Taylor Street.

Patriotism and loyalty to the country were also values that were held by the pioneers. During WWI the community showed their patriotism by buying "Liberty Bonds." Young men volunteered to fight in WWI and WWII. The patriotism of one African American family, in particular, from Punta Gorda was outstanding. At least six of the famous Bailey Brothers served in WWII. There was at least one brother in each of the four branches of the Armed Services. One brother, Charles was a member of the Tuskegee Airmen, and another, Carl, was one of the first African American jet fighter pilots. A bronze mural at the Charlotte County Airport is dedicated to the Bailey Brothers.

THE PUNTA GORDA HERALD

October 17,1918

Our colored people are proving their patriotism in more ways than one. They have contributed liberally to the Red Cross and to Belgian relief; some of their best men are in the army and others not fit for military service are working in ammunition factories "up north"; many of them are buying Liberty Bonds and now comes St. Mark's Progressive Baptist church, of which Rev. M. L. Cherry is pastor, and puts an advertisement in this paper calling upon everybody to buy Liberty Bonds. As long as we have such people as these, there is no doubt we will beat the Huns, "horse, foot, dragoon," kaiser and all.

WHAT DID I LEARN?

1. Why was it necessary for the Punta Gorda community to be a "family"?

2. How were the African American pioneers involved in the civic affairs of Punta Gorda?

3. Who were the Tuskegee Airmen?" Write a report about their accomplishments.

Daniel C. Smith

DANIEL C. SMITH

(1865-1935)

THE PUNTA GORDA HERALD

February 10, 1921

"When Dan Smith, the local colored man, came here in 1885, there were only 15 people here of who 8 were white and 7 black. He and Sam Kenady, also colored, are the only ones of the original 15 who are left."

"Dan" Smith was one the five African American survey team that future Gov. Albert Gilchrist brought to Trabue in 1885. He was a deeply religious man who organized the first religious meeting in Punta Gorda in 1886, under a thatched hut. He was a fisherman by trade but became a businessman who bought property and sold oranges from his grove.

Dan Smith was sent to find a teacher for the Colored School. He convinced Benjamin Baker to move to Punta Gorda. Dan Smith was a very respected leader in the city of Punta Gorda.

1. What values do you believe motivated Dan Smith and helped to make him a respected leader?

THE VALUE OF EQUALITY

BELIEF: We are Americans too.

Archie Bailey, Annie Mae Haynes, and Martha Andrews organized the first NAACP branch in Punta Gorda in 1933.

When the first black and white men arrived to build the railroad and establish the town of Punta Gorda, they worked side by side. African Americans owned businesses "downtown" that served white customers and many African Americans and whites lived close together.

Between 1887 and 1891 life for African Americans all over the United States, began to change, even in Punta Gorda as "Jim Crow" laws were passed. Jim Crow laws were state and local laws that required racial segregation or the separation of black and white people in all public places. These laws meant that African Americans could not go freely like whites into schools, restaurants, hospitals, or other public places. Signs that read "Whites Only" or "Colored" were placed over water fountains, waiting rooms, and restrooms.

In Florida, from 1885, African Americans could not go to school with whites or marry whites. From

1905, African Americans had to ride in separate railroad cars and sit in separate waiting rooms. They also could not use the public libraries, swimming pools, or beaches.

When the Plessy vs. Ferguson Supreme Court decision was made the law of the land, African Americans became "second-class" citizens. The schools were segregated and the "colored" school received much less money to support it than the white school. In 1915, the "colored citizens" of Punta Gorda held a mass meeting to protest inequalities in the funding of the colored school.

THE PUNTA GORDA HERALD

MASS MEETING OF COLORED CITIZENS

Whose Souls Breathe the Refreshing

Zephyrs of True Democracy Take Action

Punta Gorda, Fla.,

April 15th, 1919

We the colored citizens of Punta Gorda, Fla., at a mass meeting held at the A.M.E. church, to discuss the failure of the County School Board of DeSoto County to carry out its contract of seven (7) months with the teachers of our Public School, owing to the shortage of funds adopted the following resolutions.

Whereas the time has come for all races to throw off the yoke of bondage, and to have self-determination, and to enjoy the blessings of the coming World's Democracy, for which we have so liberally contributed, and whereas no nation, race or people can enjoy or demand the rights accorded to them by the provisions of their government, without an education and..

Whereas we are called upon to all our places as loyal American citizens, in the defense of the rights of the United

States, pass the same examination, keep down Bolshevism, (which can only be done by educating,) and Whereas we responded so liberally to the call of the government, through the buying of War Saving Stamps, Liberty Bonds, supporting the Red Cross Work to the last ditch, picking up The United War Workers Campaign with as much eagerness and force, and all of these were only to us as a starter and bracer for the VICTORY LOAN, which faces us and also mean to put that OVER TOP, among us.

We feel that we have not had a square deal, and our efforts to win Democracy for the world have failed in bringing that to the Colored American Citizens of this community will proceed to maintain our public school by raising through public subscription, one hundred ($100) dollars, the amount necessary, (having half of said amount in hand already) to carry out the unexpired term of the Punta Gorda Public School.

WHAT DID YOU LEARN?

1. What was "Jim Crow"? How were the African American pioneers treated during Jim Crow?

2. What was the "Plessy vs. Ferguson" decision? How did it affect African Americans?

3. What feelings and beliefs were expressed by the African American citizens of Punta Gorda in the April 15, 1919 newspaper article?

4. Why did the African American citizens of Punta Gorda raise the money for the colored school when the County would not?

5. How long did the "Jim Crow" era last? How did it come to an end?

LIVING HISTORY ASSIGNMENT

1. Did a civil rights movement take place in the community in which you live? If so, what were the issues, and who were the leaders? Write a report about the civil rights movement in Charlotte County or in your community.

2. What do you think it was like to live in a society segregated by race? Ask one of your elders to tell you about life during those times.

3. Watch the video series, "Eyes On The Prize." Talk to an elder and write a report about the civil rights movem11ent that took place in the United States.

4. The year 2014 was the 50th Anniversary of the passage of the Civil Rights Act of 1964. How do you feel the United States has changed since 1964?

THINK ABOUT IT

1. What did "success" mean to the African American pioneers who settled in Punta Gorda?

2. How did the values of the pioneers help them to have successful lives and to establish a successful community despite hardships?

3. How can the values of the African American pioneers who establish Punta Gorda help you to have a successful life?

4. If you do not live in Punta Gorda or Charlotte County, how are the stories of African American pioneers in your area similar to these of the pioneers of Punta Gorda? How are the values similar?

ABOUT THE AUTHORS

Martha R. Bireda, Ph.D. is Director of the Blanchard House Museum of African American History and Culture, located in Punta Gorda, Florida. For over 30 years, Dr. Bireda has consulted, lectured, and written about social issues related to race, gender, class, power, and culture. She is the author of over 17 books.

Dr. Bireda is a Florida Humanities Scholar. One of the programs that she offers to organizations throughout the State of Florida through the Florida Humanities Speaker Program is: "Punta Gorda: The Little Town That Unity Built." Her newest historical reenactment program is "Queen Andrews: Punta Gorda's Own."

Jaha Cummings is the founder of Blanchard House Institute. The Blanchard House Institute was established to operate in conjunction with the Blanchard House Museum's educational, research, and outreach mission. He is also the founder of Black Wall Street Trail and the Seminole Maroon Freedom Trail.

The Black Wall Street Trail is a national public-private partnership that seeks to educate learners of all generations and backgrounds on the golden age of historic African American business districts to promote economic and cultural development in local communities to inspire a new age of pride and prosperity for future generations. The Seminole Maroon Freedom Trail is a national public-private partnership across industries to build an economic and cultural trail that will honor and connect the Seminole Maroon communities in Florida, Oklahoma, Texas, Mexico, and The Bahamas as a source of pride for all Americans. The foundation of the trail is based on civic engagement and governance, entrepreneurship, heritage and culture.

Jaha served three terms as a City Councilman for the City of Punta Gorda. While serving on the City Council, he also served as Vice-Chair of the Charlotte County Tourism Development Council. He was appointed to represent Local Government on the 10-person Governor's Taskforce on Abandoned African American Cemeteries; and served as Historian for the Florida Black Caucus of Local Elected Officials (FBC-LEO).

www.ingramcontent.com/pod-product-compliance
Lightning Source LLC
LaVergne TN
LVHW091327190726
843491LV00002B/614